Joy and Power

Three Messages with One Meaning

By

Henry Van Dyke

JOY AND POWER

St. John viii. 17: If ye know these things, happy are ye if ye do them.

I ask you to think for a little while about the religion of Christ in its relation to happiness.

This is only one point in the circle of truth at the centre of which Jesus stands. But it is an important point because it marks one of the lines of power which radiate from Him. To look at it clearly and steadily is not to disregard other truths. The mariner takes the whole heavens of astronomy for granted while he shapes his course by a single star.

In the wish for happiness all men are strangely alike. In their explanations of it and in their ways of seeking it they are singularly different. Shall we think of this wish as right, or wrong; as a true star, or a will-o'-the-wisp? If it is right to wish to be happy, what are the conditions on which the fulfilment of this wish depends? These are the two questions with which I would come to Christ, seeking instruction and guidance.

I. The desire of happiness, beyond all doubt, is a natural desire. It is the law of life itself that every being seeks and strives toward the perfection of its kind, the realization of its own specific ideal in form and function, and a true harmony with its environment. Every drop of sap in the tree flows toward foliage and fruit. Every drop of blood in the bird beats toward flight and song. In a conscious being this movement toward perfection must take a conscious form. This conscious form is happiness,—the satisfaction of the vital impulse,—the rhythm of the inward life,—the melody of a heart that has found its keynote. To say that all men long for this is simply to confess that all men are human, and that their thoughts and feelings are an essential part of their life. Virtue means a completed manhood. The joyful welfare of the soul belongs to the fulness of that ideal. Holiness is wholeness. In striving to realize the true aim of our being, we find the wish for happiness implanted in the very heart of our effort.

Now what does Christ say in regard to this natural human wish? Does He say that it is an illusion? Does He condemn and deny it? Would He have accepted Goethe's definition: "religion is renunciation"?

Surely such a notion is far from the spirit of Jesus. There is nothing of the hardness of Stoicism, the coldness of Buddhism, in Christ's gospel. It is humane, sympathetic, consoling. Unrest and weariness, the fever of passion and the chill of despair, soul-solitude and heart-trouble, are the very things that He comes to cure. He begins His great discourse with a series of beatitudes. "Blessed" is the word. "Happy" is the meaning. Nine times He rings the changes on that word, like a silver bell sounding from His fair temple on the mountain-side, calling all who long for happiness to come to Him and find rest for their souls.

Christ never asks us to give up merely for the sake of giving up, but always in order to win something better. He comes not to destroy, but to fulfil,—to fill full,—to replenish life with true, inward, lasting riches. His gospel is a message of satisfaction, of attainment, of felicity. Its voice is not a sigh, but a song. Its final word is a benediction, a good-saying. "These things have I spoken unto you, that my joy might remain in you, and that your joy might be full."

If we accept His teaching we must believe that men are not wrong in wishing for happiness, but wrong in their way of seeking it. Earthly happiness,—pleasure that belongs to the senses and perishes with them,— earthly happiness is a dream and a delusion. But happiness on earth,— spiritual joy and peace, blossoming here, fruiting hereafter,—immortal happiness, is the keynote of life in Christ.

And if we come to Him, He tells us four great secrets in regard to it.

i. It is inward, and, not outward; and so it does not depend on what we have, but on what we are.

ii. It cannot be found by direct seeking, but by setting our faces toward the things from which it flows; and so we must climb the mount if we would see the vision, we must tune the instrument if we would hear the music.

iii. It is not solitary, but social; and so we can never have it without sharing it with others.

iv. It is the result of God's will for us, and not of our will for ourselves; and so we can only find it by giving our lives up, in submission and obedience, to the control of God.

> For this is peace,—to lose the lonely note
> Of self in love's celestial ordered strain:
> And this is joy,—to find one's self again
> In Him whose harmonies forever float
> Through all the spheres of song, below, above,—
> For God is music, even as God is love.

This is the divine doctrine of happiness as Christ taught it by His life and with His lips. If we want to put it into a single phrase, I know not where we shall find a more perfect utterance than in the words which have been taught us in childhood,—words so strong, so noble, so cheerful, that they summon the heart of manhood like marching-music: "Man's chief end is to glorify God and enjoy Him forever."

Let us accept without reserve this teaching of our Divine Lord and Master in regard to the possibility and the duty of happiness. It is an essential element of His gospel. The atmosphere of the New Testament is not gloom, but gladness; not despondency, but hope. The man who is not glad to be a Christian is not the right kind of a Christian.

The first thing that commended the Church of Jesus to the weary and disheartened world in the early years of her triumph, was her power to make her children happy,—happy in the midst of afflictions, happy in the release from the burden of guilt, happy in the sense of Divine Fatherhood and human brotherhood, happy in Christ's victory over sin and death, happy in the assurance of an endless life. At midnight in the prison, Paul and Silas sang praises, and the prisoners heard them. The lateral force of joy,—that was the power of the Church.

> "'Poor world,' she cried, 'so deep accurst,
> Thou runn'st from pole to pole

    To seek a draught to slake thy thirst,—
    Go seek it in thy soul.'

    * * * * *

    Tears washed the trouble from her face!
    She changed into a child!
    'Mid weeds and wrecks she stood,—a place
    Of ruin,—but she smiled!"

Much has the Church lost of that pristine and powerful joy. The furnace of civilization has withered and hardened her. She has become anxious and troubled about many things. She has sought earthly honours, earthly powers. Richer she is than ever before, and probably better organized, and perhaps more intelligent, more learned,—but not more happy. The one note that is most often missing in Christian life, in Christian service, is the note of spontaneous joy.

Christians are not as much calmer, steadier, stronger, and more cheerful than other people as they ought to be. Some Christians are among the most depressing and worryful people in the world,—the most difficult to live with. And some, indeed, have adopted a theory of spiritual ethics which puts a special value upon unhappiness. The dark, morbid spirit which mistrusts every joyful feeling, and depreciates every cheerful virtue, and looks askance upon every happy life as if there must be something wrong about it, is a departure from the beauty of Christ's teaching to follow the dark-browed philosophy of the Orient.

The religion of Jesus tells us that cheerful piety is the best piety. There is something finer than to do right against inclination; and that is to have an inclination to do right. There is something nobler than reluctant obedience; and that is joyful obedience. The rank of virtue is not measured by its disagreeableness, but by its sweetness to the heart that loves it. The real test of character is joy. For what you rejoice in, that you love. And what you love, that you are like.

I confess frankly that I have no admiration for the phrase "disinterested benevolence," to describe the main-spring of Christian morals. I do not find it in the New Testament: neither the words, nor the thing. Interested benevolence is what I find there. To do good to others is to make life interesting and find peace for our own souls. To glorify God is to enjoy Him. That was the spirit of the first Christians. Was not St. Paul a happier man than Herod? Did not St. Peter have more joy of his life than Nero? It is said of the first disciples that they "did eat their meat with gladness and singleness of heart." Not till that pristine gladness of life returns will the Church regain her early charm for the souls of men. Every great revival of Christian power—like those which came in the times of St. Francis of Assisi and of John Wesley—has been marked and heralded by a revival of Christian joy.

If we want the Church to be mighty in power to win men, to be a source of light in the darkness, a fountain of life in the wilderness, we must remember and renew, in the spirit of Christ, the relation of religion to human happiness.

II. What, then, are the conditions upon which true happiness depends? Christ tells us in the text: If ye know these things, happy are ye if ye do them.

This is the blessing with a double if. "If ye know,"—this is the knowledge which Christ gives to faith. "If ye do,"—this is the obedience which faith gives to Christ. Knowing and Doing,—these are the twin pillars, Jachin and Boaz, on which the house of happiness is built. The harmony of faith and life,—this is the secret of inward joy and power.

You remember when these words were spoken. Christ had knelt to wash the disciples' feet. Peter, in penitence and self-reproach, had hesitated to permit this lowly service of Divine love. But Christ answered by revealing the meaning of His act as a symbol of the cleansing of the soul from sin. He reminded the disciples of what they knew by faith,—that He was their Saviour and their Lord. By deed and by word He called up before them the great spiritual truths which had given new meaning to their life. He summoned them to live according to their knowledge, to act upon the truth which they believed.

I am sure that His words sweep out beyond that quiet upper room, beyond that beautiful incident, to embrace the whole spiritual life. I am sure that He is revealing to us the secret of happy living which lies at the very heart of His gospel, when He says: If ye know these things, happy are ye if ye do them.

i. "If ye know,"—there is, then, a certain kind of knowledge without which we can not be happy. There are questions arising in human nature which demand an answer. If it is denied we can not help being disappointed, restless, and sad. This is the price we have to pay for being conscious, rational creatures. If we were mere plants or animals we might go on living through our appointed years in complete indifference to the origin and meaning of our existence. But within us, as human beings, there is something that cries out and rebels against such a blind life. Man is born to ask what things mean. He is possessed with the idea that there is a significance in the world beyond that which meets his senses.

John Fiske has brought out this fact very clearly in his last book, Through Nature to God. He shows that "in the morning twilight of existence the Human Soul vaguely reached forth toward something akin to itself, not in the realm of fleeting phenomena, but in the Eternal Presence beyond." He argues by the analogy of evolution, which always presupposes a real relation between the life and the environment to which it adjusts itself, that this forth-reaching and unfolding of the soul implies the everlasting reality of religion.

The argument is good. But the point which concerns us now is simply this. The forth-reaching, questioning soul can never be satisfied if it touches only a dead wall in the darkness, if its seeking meets with the reply, "You do not know, and you never can know, and you must not try to know." This is agnosticism. It is only another way of spelling unhappiness.

"Since Christianity is not true," wrote Ernest Renan, "nothing interests me, or appears worthy my attention." That is the logical result of losing the knowledge of spiritual things,—a life without real interest, without deep worth,—a life with a broken spring.

But suppose Renan is mistaken. Suppose Christianity is true. Then the first thing that makes it precious, is that it answers our questions, and tells us the things that we must know in order to be happy.

Christianity is a revealing religion, a teaching religion, a religion which conveys to the inquiring spirit certain great and positive solutions of the problems of life. It is not silent, nor ambiguous, nor incomprehensible in its utterance. It replies to our questions with a knowledge which, though limited, is definite and sufficient. It tells us that this "order of nature, which constitutes the world's experience, is only one portion of the total universe." That the ruler of both worlds, seen and unseen, is God, a Spirit, and the Father of our spirits. That He is not distant from us nor indifferent to us, but that He has given His eternal Son Jesus Christ to be our Saviour. That His Spirit is ever present with us to help us in our conflicts with evil, in our efforts toward goodness. That He is making all things work together for good to those that love Him. That through the sacrifice of Christ every one who will may obtain the forgiveness of sins and everlasting peace. That through the resurrection of Christ all who love Him and their fellow-men shall obtain the victory over death and live forever.

Now these are doctrines. And it is just because Christianity contains such doctrines that it satisfies the need of man.

"The first and the most essential condition of true happiness," writes Professor Carl Hilty, the eminent Swiss jurist, "is a firm faith in the moral order of the world. What is the happy life? It is a life of conscious harmony with this Divine order of the world, a sense, that is to say, of God's companionship. And wherein is the profoundest unhappiness? It is in the sense of remoteness from God, issuing into incurable restlessness of heart, and finally into incapacity to make one's life fruitful or effective."

What shall we say, then, of the proposal to adapt Christianity to the needs of the world to-day by eliminating or ignoring its characteristic doctrines? You might as well propose to fit a ship for service by taking out its compass and its charts and cutting off its rudder. Make Christianity silent in regard to these great questions of spiritual existence, and you destroy its power to satisfy the heart.

What would the life of Christ mean if these deep truths on which He rested and from which He drew His strength, were uncertain or illusory? It would be the most pathetic, mournful, heartbreaking of all phantoms.

What consoling, cheering power would be left in the words of Jesus if His doctrine were blotted out and His precept left to stand alone? Try the experiment, if it may be done without irreverence: read His familiar discourses in the shadow of agnosticism.

'Blessed are the poor in spirit, for theirs is a hopeless poverty. Blessed are the pure in heart, for they know not whether they shall see God. Blessed are ye when men shall revile you and persecute you, for ye have no promise of a heavenly reward.

'Enter into thy closet and when thou hast shut the door, keep silence, for thou canst not tell whether there is One to hear thy voice in secret. Take no thought for the morrow, for thou knowest not whether there is a Father who careth for thee.

'God is unknown, and they that worship Him must worship Him in ignorance and doubt. No man hath ascended up into heaven, neither hath any man come down from heaven, for the Son of Man hath never been in heaven. That which is born of the flesh is flesh, and that which is born of the spirit is a dream. Man shall not live by bread alone, neither shall he listen for any word from the mouth of God. I proceeded forth and came from darkness, I came of myself, I know not who sent me. My sheep hear my voice, and I know them, and they follow me, but I can not give unto them eternal life, for they shall perish and death shall pluck them out of my hand. Let not your heart be troubled; ye believe not in God, ye need not believe in me. Keep my commandments, and I will not pray for you, and ye shall abide without a Comforter. In the world ye shall have tribulation, but be of good cheer, for ye know not whether there is a world to come. I came forth from darkness into the world, and again I leave the world and return to darkness. Peace I leave with you. If ye loved me ye would rejoice because I said, I go into darkness, and where I am there shall ye be also.'

Is it conceivable that any suffering, sorrowing human soul should be comforted and strengthened by such a message as this? Could it possibly be called a gospel, glad tidings of great joy to all people?

And yet what has been omitted here from the words of Christ? Nothing but what men call doctrines: the personality of God, the divinity of Christ, the Atonement, the presence and power of the Holy Spirit, the sovereignty of the Heavenly Father, the truth of the divine revelation, the reality of the heavenly world, the assurance of immortal life. But it is just from these doctrines that the teaching of Jesus draws its peculiar power to comfort and inspire. They are the rays of light which disperse the gloom of uncertainty. They are the tones of celestial music which fill the heart of man with good cheer.

Let us never imagine that we can strengthen Christianity by leaving out the great doctrines which have given it life and power. Faith is not a mere matter of feeling. It is the acceptance of truth, positive, unchanging, revealed truth, in regard to God and the world, Christ and the soul, duty and immortality. The first appeal to faith lies in the clearness and vividness, the simplicity and joy, with which this truth is presented.

There has not been too much preaching of doctrine in this age. There has been too little. And what there has been, has been too dull and cold and formal, too vague and misty, too wavering and uncertain.

What the world wants and waits for to-day is a strong, true, vital preaching of doctrine. The Church must realize anew the precious value of the truths which Christ has given her. She must not conceal them or cast them away; she must bring them out into the light, press them home upon the minds and hearts of men. She must simplify her statement of them, so that men can understand what they mean. She must not be content with repeating them in the language of past centuries. She must translate them into the language of to-day. First century texts will never wear out because they are inspired. But seventeenth century sermons grow obsolete because they are not inspired. Texts from the Word of God, preaching in the words of living men,—that is what we need.

We must think about the doctrines of Christianity more earnestly and profoundly. We must renew our Christian evidences, as an army fits itself with new weapons. The old-fashioned form of the "argument from design in nature" has gone out with the old-fashioned books of science which it used. But there is a new and more wonderful proof of God's presence in the world,—the argument from moral ends in evolution. Every real advance of science makes the intelligent order of the universe more sublimely clear. Every century of human experience confirms the Divine claims and adds to the Divine triumphs of Jesus Christ. Social progress has followed to a hair's breadth the lines of His gospel; and He lays His hand to-day with heavenly wisdom on the social wants that still trouble us, "the social lies that warp us from the living truth." Christ's view of life and the world is as full of sweet reasonableness now as it was in the first century. Every moral step that man has taken upward has brought a wider, clearer vision of his need of such a religion as that which Christ teaches.

Let not the Church falter and blush for her doctrines. Let her not turn and go down the hill of knowledge to defend her position in the valley of ignorance. Let her go up the hill, welcoming every wider outlook, rejoicing in every new discovery, gathering fresh evidences of the truths which man must believe concerning God and new motives to the duties which God requires of man.

But in doing this we must put the emphasis of our preaching to-day where it belongs, where Christ puts it, on the doctrines that are most important to human life and happiness. We can afford to let the fine metaphysical distinctions of theology rest for a while, and throw all our force on the central, fundamental truths which give steadiness and courage and cheer to the heart of man. I will not admit that it makes no difference to a man of this age whether or not he believes in the personal God and the Divine Christ. If he really believes, it makes all the difference between spiritual strength and spiritual weakness, between optimism and pessimism. I will not admit that it makes no difference to a learned scholar or a simple labourer to-day whether he accepts or ignores the doctrine of the atonement, the doctrine of personal immortality. If he knows that Christ died for him, that there is a future beyond the grave, it makes all the difference between despair and hope, between misery and consolation, between the helpless frailty of a being that is puffed out like a candle, and the joyful power of an endless life.

My brethren, we must work and pray for a true revival of Christian doctrine in our age. We must deepen our own hold upon the truths which Christ has taught us. We must preach them more simply, more confidently, more reasonably, more earnestly. We must draw from them the happiness and the help, the comfort and the inspiration, that they have to give to the souls of men. But most of all, we must keep them in close and living touch with the problems of daily duty and experience. For no doctrine, however high, however true, can make men happy until it is translated into life.

ii. Here is the second if, on which the power of religion to confer happiness depends: If ye know, happy are ye if ye do these things.

Between the knowing and the doing there is a deep gulf. Into that abyss the happiness of many a man slips, and is lost. There is no peace, no real and lasting felicity for a human life until the gulf is closed, and the continent of conduct meets the continent of creed, edge to edge, lip to lip, firmly joined forever.

It is not a blessing to know the things that Christ teaches, and then go on living as if they were false or doubtful. It is a trouble, a torment, a secret misery. To know that God is our Father, and yet to withhold our love and service from Him; to know that Christ died for us, and yet to deny Him and refuse to follow Him; to know that there is an immortal life, and yet to waste and lose our souls in the pursuit of sensual pleasure and such small portion of the world as we may hope to gain,—surely that is the deepest of all unhappiness.

But the right kind of knowing carries in its heart the doing of the truth. And the right kind of doing leads to a fuller and happier knowing. "If any man will do God's will," declares Christ, "he shall know of the doctrine."

Let a man take the truth of the Divine Fatherhood and begin to conform his life to its meaning. Let him give up his anxious worryings, his murmurings, his complainings, and trust himself completely to his Father's care. Let him do his work from day to day as well as he can and leave the results to God. Let him come to his Father every day and confess his faults and ask for help and guidance. Let him try to obey and please God for love's sake. Let him take refuge from the trials and confusions and misunderstandings of the world, from the wrath of men and the strife of tongues, in the secret of his Father's presence. Surely if he learns the truth thus, by doing it, he will find happiness.

Or take the truth of immortality. Let a man live now in the light of the knowledge that he is to live forever. How it will deepen and strengthen the meaning of his existence, lift him above petty cares and ambitions, and make the things that are worth while precious to his heart! Let him really set his affections on the spiritual side of life, let him endure afflictions patiently because he knows that they are but for a moment, let him think more of the soul than of the body, let him do good to his fellow-men in order to make them sharers of his immortal hope, let him purify his love and friendship that they may be fit for the heavenly life. Surely the man who does these things will be happy. It will be with him as with Lazarus, in Robert Browning's poem, "The Epistle of Karshish." Others will look at him with wonder and say:

> "Whence has the man the balm that brightens all?
> This grown man eyes the world now like a child."

Yes, my brethren, this is the sure result of following out the doctrines of Christ in action, of living the truths that He teaches,—a simple life, a childlike life, a happy life. And this also the Church needs to-day, as well as a true revival of doctrine.

A revival of simplicity, a revival of sincerity, a revival of work: this will restore unto us the joy of salvation. And with the joy of salvation will come a renewal and expansion of power.

The inconsistency of Christians is the stronghold of unbelief. The lack of vital joy in the Church is the chief cause of indifference in the world. The feeble energy, the faltering and reluctant spirit, the weariness in well-doing with which too many believers impoverish and sadden their own hearts, make other men question the reality and value of religion and turn away from it in cool neglect.

What, then, is the duty of the Church? What must she do to win the confidence of the world? What is the best way for her to "prove her doctrine all divine"?

First, she must increase her labours in the love of men: second, she must practice the simple life, deepening her trust in God.

Suppose that a fresh flood of energy, brave, cheerful, joyous energy, should be poured into all the forms of Christian work. Suppose that Foreign Missions and Home Missions should no longer have to plead and beg for support, but that plenty of money should come flowing in to send out every missionary that wants to go, and that plenty of the strongest and best young men should dedicate their lives to the ministry of Christ, and that every household where His gospel is believed should find its highest honour and its greatest joy in helping to extend His kingdom.

And then suppose that the Christian life, in its daily manifestation, should come to be marked and known by simplicity and happiness. Suppose that the followers of Jesus should really escape from bondage to the evil spirits of avarice and luxury which infect and torment so much of our complicated, tangled, artificial, modern life. Suppose that instead of increasing their wants and their desires, instead of loading themselves down on life's journey with so many bags and parcels and boxes of superfluous luggage and bric-a-brac that they are forced to sit down by the roadside and gasp for breath, instead of wearing themselves out in the dusty ways of ostentation and vain show or embittering their hearts because they can not succeed in getting into the weary race of wealth and fashion,—suppose instead of all this, they should turn to quiet ways, lowly pleasures, pure and simple joys, "plain living and high thinking." Suppose they should truly find and show their happiness in the knowledge that God loves them and Christ died for them and heaven is sure, and so set their hearts free to rejoice in life's common mercies, the light of the sun, the blue of the sky, the splendour of the sea, the peace of the everlasting hills, the song of birds, the sweetness of flowers, the wholesome savour of good food, the delights of action and motion, the refreshment of sleep, the charm of music, the blessings of human love and friendship,—rejoice in all these without fear or misgiving, because they come from God and because Christ has sanctified them all by His presence and touch.

Suppose, I say, that such a revival of the joy of living in Christ and working for Christ should silently sweep over the Church in the Twentieth Century. What would happen? Great would be the peace of her children. Greater still would be their power.

This is the message which I have to bring to you, my brethren, in this General Assembly of the Presbyterian Church. You may wonder that it is not more distinctive, more ecclesiastical, more specially adapted to the peculiarities of our own denomination. You may think that it is a message which could just as well be brought to any other Church on any other occasion. With all my heart I hope that is true. The things that I care for most in our Church are not those which divide us from other Christians but those which unite us to them. The things that I love most in Christianity are those which give it power to save and satisfy, to console and cheer, to inspire and bless human hearts and lives. The thing that I desire most for Presbyterianism is that it should prove its mission and extend its influence in the world by making men happy in the knowing and the doing of the things which Christ teaches.

The Church that the Twentieth Century will hear most gladly and honour most sincerely will have two marks. It will be the Church that teaches most clearly and strongly the truths that Jesus taught. It will be the Church that finds most happiness in living the simple life and doing good in the world.

THE BATTLE OF LIFE

Romans vii. 21: Overcome evil with good.

The Battle of Life is an ancient phrase consecrated by use in Commencement Orations without number. Two modern expressions have taken their place beside it in our own day: the Strenuous Life, and the Simple Life.

Each of these phrases has its own significance and value. It is when they are overemphasized and driven to extremes that they lose their truth and become catch-words of folly. The simple life which blandly ignores all care and conflict, soon becomes flabby and invertebrate, sentimental and gelatinous. The strenuous life which does everything with set jaws and clenched fists and fierce effort, soon becomes strained and violent, a prolonged nervous spasm.

Somewhere between these two extremes must lie the golden mean: a life that has strength and simplicity, courage and calm, power and peace. But how can we find this golden line and live along it? Some truth there must be in the old phrase which speaks of life as a battle. No conflict, no character. Without strife, a weak life. But what is the real meaning of the battle? What is the vital issue at stake? What are the things worth fighting for? In what spirit, with what weapons, are we to take our part in the warfare?

There is an answer to these questions in the text: *Overcome evil with good.* The man who knows this text by heart, knows the secret of a life that is both strenuous and simple. For here we find the three things that we need most: a call to the real battle of life; a plan for the right campaign; and a promise of final victory.

I. Every man, like the knight in the old legend, is born on a field of battle. But the warfare is not carnal, it is spiritual. Not the east against the west, the north against the south, the "Haves" against the "Have-nots"; but the evil against the good,—that is the real conflict of life.

The attempt to deny or ignore this conflict has been the stock in trade of every false doctrine that has befogged and bewildered the world since the days of Eden. The fairy tale that the old serpent told to Eve is a poetic symbol of the lie fundamental,—the theory that sin does not mean death, because it has no real existence and makes no real difference. This ancient falsehood has an infinite wardrobe of disguises.

You will find it pranked out in philosophic garb in the doctrines of those who teach that all things are linked together by necessity of nature or Divine will, and that nothing could ever have happened otherwise than just as it has come to pass. Such a theory of the universe blots out all difference between good and evil except in name. It leaves the fence-posts standing, but it takes away the rails, and throws everything into one field of the inevitable.

You will find the same falsehood in a more crude form in the popular teachings of what men call "the spirit of the age," the secular spirit. According to these doctrines the problem of civilization is merely a problem of ways and means. If society were better organized, if wealth were more equally distributed, if laws were changed, or perhaps abolished, all would be well. If everybody had a full dinner-pail, nobody need care about an empty heart. Human misery the secular spirit recognizes, but it absolutely ignores the fact that nine-tenths of human misery comes from human sin.

You will find the same falsehood disguised in sentimental costume in the very modern comedy of Christian Science, which dresses the denial of evil in pastoral garb of white frock and pink ribbons, like an innocent shepherdess among her lambs. "Evil is nothing," says this wonderful Science. "It does not really exist. It is an illusion of mortal mind. Shut your eyes and it will vanish."

Yes, but open your eyes again and you will see it in the same place, in the same form, doing the same work. A most persistent nothing, a most powerful nothing! Not the shadow cast by the good, but the cloud that hides the sun and casts the shadow. Not the "silence implying sound," but the discord breaking the harmony. Evil is as real as the fire that burns you, as the flood that drowns you. Evil is as real as the typhoid germ that you can put under a microscope and see it squirm and grow. Evil is negative,—yes, but it is a real negative,—as real as darkness, as real as death.

There are two things in every human heart which bear witness to the existence and reality of evil: first, our judgments of regret, and second, our judgments of condemnation.

How often we say to ourselves, "Would that this had not come to pass!" How often we feel in regard to our own actions, "Would that I had done differently!" This is the judgment of regret; and it is a silent witness of the heart to the conviction that some things are not inevitable. It is the confession that a battle has been lost which might have been won. It is the acknowledgment that things which are, but are not right, need not have been, if we and our fellow-men had seen more clearly and followed more faithfully the guiding star of the good.

And then, out of the judgment of regret, springs the deeper judgment of condemnation. If the failure in duty was not inevitable, then it was base. The false word, the unjust deed, the foul action, seen as a surrender to evil, appears hateful and guilty. It deserves the indignation and the shame which attach to all treason. And the spirit which lies behind all these forms of disloyalty to the good,—the spirit which issues in selfishness and sensuality, cruelty and lust, intemperance and covetousness,—this animating spirit of evil which works against the Divine will and mars the peace and order of the universe is the great Adversary against whom we must fight for our own lives and the life of the world.

All around us lies his dark, secret kingdom, tempting, threatening, assaulting the soul. To ignore it, is to walk blindfold among snares and pitfalls. Try if you will to shut it out, by wrapping your heart in dreams of beauty and joy, living in the fair regions of art or philosophy, reading only the books which speak of evil as if it did not exist or were only another form of goodness. Soon you will be shaken out of the dream into the reality. You will come into contact with evil so close, so loathsome that you can not deny it. You will see that it has its soldiers, its servants, its emissaries, as ardent and enthusiastic in its cause as if they were serving the noblest of masters. It inspires literature and supports newspapers; now intelligent and cultured, drawing the arts into its service; now coarse and vulgar, with pictures that shock the taste as much as they debase the conscience. It wins adherents and turns them into advocates. It organizes the dealers in drunkenness and debauchery into powerful societies for mutual protection. It creates lobbies and controls legislatures. It corrupts the government of great cities and rots out the social life of small towns. Even when its outward manifestations are repressed and its grosser forms resisted, it steals its way into men's hearts, eating out the roots of human trust and brotherhood and kindness, and filling the air with gossip and spite, envy, malice and all uncharitableness.

I am glad that since we have to live in a world where evil exists, we have a religion which does not bandage our eyes. The first thing that we need to have religion do for us is to teach us to face the facts. No man can come into touch with the Divine personality of Jesus Christ, no man can listen to His teaching, without feeling that the distinction between good and evil to Him is vital and everlasting. The choice between them is to Him the great choice. The conflict between them is to Him the great conflict. Evil is the one thing that God has never willed. Good is the one thing that He wills forever. Evil is first and last a rebellion against His will. He is altogether on the side of good. Much that is, is contrary to His will. There is a mighty strife going on, a battle with eternal issues, but not an eternal battle. The evil that is against Him shall be cast out and shall perish. The good that overcomes the evil shall live forever. And those who yield their lives to God and receive His righteousness in Christ are made partakers of everlasting life.

This is the teaching of Jesus: and I thank God for the honesty and virility of His religion which makes us face the facts and calls us to take a man's part in the real battle of life.

II. But what is the plan of campaign which Christianity sets before us? In what spirit and with what weapons are we to enter the great conflict against the evil that is in the world?

The natural feeling of the heart in the presence of evil is wrath, and the natural weapon of wrath is force. To punish crime, to avenge wrong, to put down wickedness with a strong hand,—that is the first impulse of every one who has the instincts of manhood.

And as this is natural, so it is, also, within a certain sphere needful, and to a certain extent useful. Armies and navies exist, at least in theory, to prevent injustice among nations. Laws are made to punish wrong-doers. Courts, police-forces, and prisons are maintained to suppress evil with power.

But while we recognize this method of dealing with evil as useful to a certain extent and necessary within a certain sphere, we must remember that it has its strict limitations.

First, it belongs to the state and not to the individual. When the private man assumes to punish evil with force he sanctions lynch-law, which is a terror to the innocent as well as to the guilty. Then we have the blood-feud and the vendetta, mob-rule and anarchy.

Second, the suppression of evil by force is only a temporary relief, a protection for the moment. It does not touch the root of the matter. You send the murderer out of the world by a regulated flash of lightning. But you do not send murder out of the world. To do that you must reach and change the heart of Cain. You put the thief in prison, but when he comes out he will be ready to steal again, unless you can purify his conscience and control his will. You assault and overthrow some system of misgovernment, and "turn the rascals out." But unless you have something better to substitute, all you have done is to make room for a new set of rascals,—a new swarm of mosquitoes with fresh appetites and larger capacities.

Third, the method of fighting evil with force on its own ground often has a bad effect on those who follow it. Wrestle with a chimney-sweep and you will need a bath. Throw back the mud that is thrown at you, and you will have dirty hands. Answer Shimei when he curses you and you will echo his profanity. Many a man has entered a crusade against intemperance and proved himself as intemperate in his language as other men are in their potations. Many a man has attacked a bad cause with righteous indignation and ended in a personal squabble with most unrighteous anger.

No, my brother-men, the best way to fight against evil is not to meet it on its own ground with its own weapons. There is a nobler method of warfare, a divine plan of campaign given to us in the religion of Christ. Overcome evil with good. This is the secret of the battle of life.

Evil is potent not so much because it has command of money and the "big battalions," but because it has control of the hearts of men. It spreads because human hearts are lying fallow and ready to welcome the seeds of all kinds of weeds. It persists because too much of what we call virtue is negative, and selfish, and frost-bound,—cold storage virtue,—the poor piety which terminates in a trembling anxiety to save our own souls.

The way to counteract and conquer evil in the world is to give our own hearts to the dominion of good, and work the works of God while it is day. The strongest of all obstacles to the advance of evil is a clean and generous man, doing his duty from day to day, and winning others, by his cheerful fidelity, to serve the same Master. Diseases are not the only things that are contagious. Courage is contagious. Kindness is contagious. Manly integrity is contagious. All the positive virtues, with red blood in their veins, are contagious. The heaviest blow that you can strike at the kingdom of evil is just to follow the advice which the dying Sir Walter Scott gave to his son-in-law, Lockhart: "Be a good man." And if you want to know how, there is but one perfect and supreme example,—the life of Him who not only did no evil but went about doing good.

Now take that thought of fighting evil with good and apply it to our world and to ourselves.

Here are monstrous evils and vices in society. Let intemperance be the type of them all, because so many of the others are its children. Drunkenness ruins more homes and wrecks more lives than war. How shall we oppose it? I do not say that we shall not pass resolutions and make laws against it. But I do say that we can never really conquer the evil in this way. I hold with Phillips Brooks that "all prohibitory measures are negative. That they have their uses no one can doubt. That they have their limits is just as clear."

The stronghold of intemperance lies in the vacancy and despair of men's minds. The way to attack it is to make the sober life beautiful and happy and full of interest. Teach your boys how to work, how to read, how to play, you fathers, before you send them to college, if you want to guard them against the temptations of strong drink and the many shames and sorrows that go with it. Make the life of your community cheerful and pleasant and interesting, you reformers, provide men with recreation which will not harm them, if you want to take away the power of the gilded saloon and the grimy boozing-ken. Parks and play-grounds, libraries and music-rooms, clean homes and cheerful churches,—these are the efficient foes of intemperance. And the same thing is true of gambling and lubricity and all the other vices which drag men down by the lower side of their nature because the higher side has nothing to cling to, nothing to sustain it and hold it up.

What are you going to do, my brother-men, for this higher side of human life? What contribution are you going to make of your strength, your time, your influence, your money, your self, to make a cleaner, fuller, happier, larger, nobler life possible for some of your fellow-men? I do not ask how you are going to do it. You may do it in business, in the law, in medicine, in the ministry, in teaching, in literature. But this is the question: What are you going to give personally to make the human life of the place where you do your work, purer, stronger, brighter, better, and more worth living? That will be your best part in the warfare against vice and crime.

The positive method is the only efficient way to combat intellectual error and spiritual evil. False doctrines are never argued out of the world. They are pushed back by the incoming of the truth as the darkness is pushed back by the dawn. Phillips Brooks was right. It is not worth while to cross the street to break a man's idol. It is worth while to cross the ocean to tell him about God. The skilful fencer who attacks your doubts and drives you from corner to corner of unbelief and leaves you at last in doubt whether you doubt or not, does you a certain service. He gives you exercise, takes the conceit out of you. But the man who lays hold of the real faith that is hidden underneath your doubt,—the silent longing for God and goodness, the secret attraction that draws your heart toward Jesus Christ as the only one who has the words of everlasting life,—the man who takes hold of this buried faith and quickens it and makes you dare to try to live by it,—ah, that is the man who helps you indeed. My brothers, if any of you are going to be preachers remember this. What we men need is not so much an answer to our doubts, as more nourishment for our faith.

The positive method is the only way of victory in our struggle with the evil that dwells in our own nature and besets our own hearts. The reason why many men fail, is because they thrust the vice out and then forget to lay hold on the virtue. They evict the unclean spirit and leave a vacant house. To cease to do evil is important, but to learn to do good is far more important. Reformation never saved a man. Transformation is the only way. And to be transformed, a man must welcome the Spirit of Good, the Holy Spirit, into his heart, and work with Him every day, doing the will of God.

There are two ways of fighting fever. One is to dose the sick people with quinine and keep the fever down. The other is to drain the marshes, and purify the water, and cleanse the houses, and drive the fever out. Try negative, repressive religion, and you may live, but you will be an invalid. Try positive, vital religion, and you will be well.

There is an absorption of good that guards the soul against the infection of evil. There is a life of fellowship with Christ that can pass through the furnace of the world without the smell of fire on its garments,—a life that is full of interest as His was, being ever about His Father's business; a life that is free and generous and blessed, as His was, being spent in doing good, and refreshed by the sense of God's presence and approval.

Last summer, I saw two streams emptying into the sea. One was a sluggish, niggardly rivulet, in a wide, fat, muddy bed; and every day the tide came in and drowned out that poor little stream, and filled it with bitter brine. The other was a vigorous, joyful, brimming mountain-river, fed from unfailing springs among the hills; and all the time it swept the salt water back before it and kept itself pure and sweet; and when the tide came in, it only made the fresh water rise higher and gather new strength by the delay; and ever the living stream poured forth into the ocean its tribute of living water,—the symbol of that influence which keeps the ocean of life from turning into a Dead Sea of wickedness.

My brother-men, will you take that living stream as a type of your life in the world? The question for you is not what you are going to get out of the world, but what you are going to give to the world. The only way to meet and overcome the inflowing tide of evil is to roll against it the outflowing river of good.

My prayer for you is that you may receive from Christ not only the watchword of this nobler life, but also the power to fulfil it.

THE GOOD OLD WAY

Jeremiah vi. 16. Stand ye in the ways and see; and ask for the old paths, where is the good way; and walk therein, and ye shall find rest for your souls.

This advice was given to people who were in peril and perplexity. The kingdom of Judah was threatened with destruction, which could be averted only by wise and prompt action. But the trouble was to decide in which direction that action should be taken. The nation was divided into loud parties, and these parties into noisy wings. Every man had a theory of his own, or a variation of some other man's theory.

Some favoured an alliance with the East; some preferred the friendship of the West; others, a course of diplomatic dalliance; a few stood out for honest independence. Some said that what the country needed was an increase of wealth; some held that a splendid and luxurious court like that of Pharaoh or Nebuchadnezzar would bring prosperity; others maintained that the troubles of the land could be healed only by a return to "simpler manners, purer laws." Among the nobility and their followers all kinds of novelties in the worship of idols were in fashion and new gods were imported every season. The philosophers cultivated a discreet indifference to all religious questions. The prophets taught that the only salvation for the nation lay in the putting away of idolatry and the revival of faith in the living and true God.

Judah was like a man standing at the cross-roads, on a stormy night, with all the guide-posts blown down. Meantime the Babylonian foe was closing in around Jerusalem, and it was necessary to do something, or die.

The liberty of choice was an embarrassment. The minds of men alternated between that rash haste which is ready to follow any leader who makes noise enough, and that skeptical spirit which doubts whether any line of action can be right because so many lines are open. Into this atmosphere of fever and fog came the word of the prophet. Let us consider what it means.

Stand ye in the ways and see: that means deliberation. When you are at a junction it is no time to shut your eyes and run at full speed. Where there are so many ways some of them are likely to be wrong. A turning-point is the place for prudence and forethought.

Ask for the old paths, what is the good way: that means guidance. No man is forced to face the problems of life alone. Other men have tried the different ways. Peace, prosperity, victory have been won by the nation in former times. Inquire of the past how these blessings were secured. Look for the path which has already led to safety and happiness. Let history teach you which among all these crossing ways is the best to follow.

And walk therein: that means action. When you have deliberated, when you have seen the guiding light upon the way of security and peace, then go ahead. Prudence is worthless unless you put it into practice. When in doubt do nothing; but as long as you do nothing you will be in doubt. Never man or nation was saved by inaction. The only way out of danger is the way into work. Gird up your loins, trembling Judah, and push along your chosen path, steadily, bravely, strenuously, until you come to your promised rest.

Now I am sure this was good counsel that the prophet gave to his people in the days of perplexity. It would have been well for them if they had followed it I am sure it is also good counsel for us, a word of God to steady us and stimulate us amid life's confusions. Let me make it a personal message to you.

Stand in the ways: Ask for the good way: Walk therein:—Deliberation, Guidance, Action,—Will you take these words with you, and try to make them a vital influence in your life?

I. First, I ask you to stand in the ways and see. I do not mean to say that you have not already been doing this to a certain extent. The great world is crossed by human footsteps which make paths leading in all directions. Men travel through on different ways; and I suppose some of you have noticed the fact, and thought a little about it.

There is the way of sensuality. Those who walk in it take appetite as their guide. Their main object in life is to gratify their physical desires. Some of them are delicate, and some of them are coarse. That is a matter of temperament. But all of them are hungry. That is a matter of principle. Whether they grub in the mire for their food like swine, or browse daintily upon the tree-tops like the giraffe, the question of life for those who follow this way is the same. "How much can we hold? How can we obtain the most pleasure for these five senses of ours before they wear out?" And the watchword of their journey is, "Let us eat and drink and be merry, for we do not expect to die to-morrow."

There is the way of avarice. Those who follow it make haste to be rich. The almighty dollar rolls before them along the road, and they chase it. Some of them plod patiently along the highway of toil. Others are always leaping fences and trying to find short cuts to wealth. But they are alike in this: whatever they do by way of avocation, the real vocation of their life is to make money. If they fail, they are hard and bitter; if they succeed they are hard and proud. But they all bow down to the golden calf, and their motto is, "Lay up for yourselves treasures upon earth."

There is the way of social ambition. Those who walk in it have their eyes fixed on various prizes, such as titles of honour, public office, large acquaintance with prosperous people, the reputation of leading the fashion. But the real satisfaction that they get out of it all is simply the feeling of notoriety, the sense of belonging to a circle to which ordinary people are not admitted and to whose doings the world, just for this reason, pays envious attention. This way is less like a road than like a ladder. Most of the people who are on it are "climbers."

There are other ways, less clearly marked, more difficult to trace,—the way of moral indifference, the way of intellectual pride, the way of hypocrisy, the way of indecision. This last is not a single road; it is a net-work of sheep-tracks, crossing and recrossing the great highways, leading in every direction, and ending nowhere. The men who wander in these aimless paths go up and down through the world, changing their purposes, following one another blindly, forever travelling but never arriving at the goal of their journey.

Through all this tangle there runs another way,—the path of faith and duty. Those who walk in it believe that life has a meaning, the fulfilment of God's will, and a goal, the attainment of perfect harmony with Him. They try to make the best of themselves in soul and body by training and discipline. They endeavour to put their talents to the noblest use in the service of their fellow-men, and to unfold their faculties to the highest joy and power in the life of the Spirit. They seek an education to fit them for work, and they do their work well because it is a part of their education. They respect their consciences, and cherish their ideals. They put forth an honest effort to be good and to do good and to make the world better. They often stumble. They sometimes fall. But, take their life from end to end, it is a faithful attempt to walk in "the way of righteousness, which is the way of peace."

Such are some of the ways that lead through the world. And they are all open to us. We can travel by the road that pleases us. Heredity gives us our outfit. Environment supplies our company. But when we come to the cross-roads, the question is, "Boy, which way will you ride?"

Deliberation is necessary, unless we wish to play a fool's part. No amount of energy will take the place of thought. A strenuous life, with its eyes shut, is a kind of wild insanity. A drifting life, with its eyes open, is a kind of mild idiocy.

The real question is, "How will you live? After what rule and pattern? Along what way? Toward what end?"

Will you let chance answer that question for you? Will you let yourself be led blindfold by the first guide that offers, or run stupidly after the crowd without asking whither they are going? You would not act so in regard to the shortest earthly journey. You would not rush into the railway station and jump aboard of the first train you saw, without looking at the sign-boards. Surely if there is anything in regard to which we need to exercise deliberation, it is the choice of the way that we are to take through the world. You have thought a good deal about what business, what profession you are to follow. Think more deeply, I beg you, about how you are to follow it and what you are to follow it for. Stand in the ways, and see.

II. Second, I earnestly advise you to ask for the old paths, where is the good way.

I do not regard this as a mere counsel of conservatism, an unqualified commendation of antiquity. True, it implies that the good way will not be a new discovery, a track that you and I strike out for ourselves. Among the paths of conduct, that which is entirely original is likely to be false, and that which is true is likely to have some footprints on it. When a man comes to us with a scheme of life which he has made all by himself, we may safely say to him, as the old composer said to the young musician who brought him a symphony of the future, "It is both new and beautiful; but that which is new is not beautiful, and that which is beautiful is not new."

But this is by no means the same as saying that everything ancient is therefore beautiful and true, or that all the old ways are good. The very point of the text is that we must discriminate among antiquities,—a thing as necessary in old chairs and old books as in old ways.

Evil is almost, if not quite, as ancient as good. Folly and wisdom, among men at least, are twins, and we can not distinguish between them by the grey hairs. Adam's way was old enough; and so was the way of Cain, and of Noah's vile son, and of Lot's lewd daughters, and of Balaam, and of Jezebel, and of Manasseh. Judas Iscariot was as old as St. John. Ananias and Sapphira were of the same age with St. Peter and St. Paul.

What we are to ask for is not simply the old way, but that one among the old ways which has been tested and tried and proved to be the good way. The Spirit of Wisdom tells us that we are not to work this way out by logarithms, or evolve it from our own inner consciousness, but to learn what it is by looking at the lives of other men and marking the lessons which they teach us. Experience has been compared to the stern-light of a ship which shines only on the road that has been traversed. But the stern-light of a ship that sails before you is a head-light to you.

You do not need to try everything for yourself in order to understand what it means. The writer of Ecclesiastes tells us that he gave his heart to know madness and folly; and that it was all vanity and vexation of spirit. It will be a wise economy for us to accept his lesson without paying his tuition-fee over again.

It is perfectly safe for a man to take it as a fact that fire burns, without putting his hand into the flame. He does not need to try perilous experiments with his own soul in order to make sure that lust defiles, that avarice hardens, that frivolity empties, that selfishness cankers the heart. He may understand the end of the way of sensuality by looking at any old pleasure-seeker,

"Gray, and gap-toothed, and lean as death,"

mumbling the dainties that he can no longer enjoy, and glowering with bleared eyes at the indulgences which now mock him even while they tempt him. The goal of the path of covetousness may be discerned in the face of any old money-worshipper; keeping guard over his piles of wealth, like a surly watch-dog; or, if perchance he has failed, haunting the places where fortune has deceived him, like an unquiet ghost.

Inquire and learn; consider and discern. There need be no doubt about the direction of life's various ways.

Which are the nations that have been most peaceful and noble and truly prosperous? Those that have followed pride and luxury and idolatry? Or those that have cherished sobriety and justice, and acknowledged the Divine law of righteousness?

Which are the families that have been most serene and pure and truly fortunate? Those in which there has been no discipline, no restraint, no common faith, no mutual love? Or those in which sincere religion has swayed life to its stern and gracious laws, those in which parents and children have walked together to the House of God, and knelt together at His altar, and rejoiced together in His service?

I tell you, my brother-men, it has become too much the fashion in these latter days to sneer and jeer at the old-fashioned ways of the old-fashioned American household. Something too much of iron there may have been in the Puritan's temper; something too little of sunlight may have come in through the narrow windows of his house. But that house had foundations, and the virile virtues lived in it. There were plenty of red corpuscles in his blood, and his heart beat in time with the eternal laws of right, even though its pulsations sometimes seemed a little slow and heavy. It would be well for us if we could get back into the old way, which proved itself to be the good way, and maintain, as our fathers did, the sanctity of the family, the sacredness of the marriage-vow, the solemnity of the mutual duties binding parents and children together. From the households that followed this way have come men that could rule themselves as well as their fellows, women that could be trusted as well as loved. Read the history of such families, and you will understand the truth of the poet's words:—

> "Self-reverence, self-knowledge, self-control,—
> These three alone lead life to sovereign power."

Look around you in the world and see what way it is that has brought your fellow-men to peace and quietness of heart, to security and honour of life. Is it the way of unbridled self-indulgence, of unscrupulous greed, of aimless indolence? Or is it the way of self-denial, of cheerful industry, of fair dealing, of faithful service? If true honour lies in the respect and grateful love of one's fellow-men, if true success lies in a contented heart and a peaceful conscience, then the men who have reached the highest goal of life are those who have followed most closely the way to which Jesus Christ points us and in which He goes before us.

III. Walk therein and ye shall find rest for your souls. Right action brings rest.

Rest! Rest! How that word rings like a sweet bell through the turmoil of our age. We are rushing to and fro, destroying rest in our search for it. We drive our automobiles from one place to another, at furious speed, not knowing what we shall do when we get there. We make haste to acquire new possessions, not knowing how we shall use them when they are ours. We are in a fever of new discoveries and theories, not knowing how to apply them when they are made. We feed ourselves upon novel speculations until our heads swim with the vertigo of universal knowledge which changes into the paresis of universal doubt.

But in the hours of silence, the Spirit of Wisdom whispers a secret to our hearts. Rest depends upon conduct. The result of your life depends upon your choosing the good way and walking in it.

And to you I say, my brother-men, choose Christ, for He is the Way. All the strength and sweetness of the best possible human life are embodied in Him. All the truth that is needed to inspire and guide man to noble action and fine character is revealed in Him. He is the one Master altogether worthy to be served and followed. Take His yoke upon you and learn of Him, and ye shall find rest unto your souls.